Contents
Grade 3

ISBN: 978-1-927042-06-9

S0-ELM-413

NUNAVUT,
Canada's Newest Territory

Originally, Canada was made up of ten provinces and two northern territories called the Yukon and the Northwest Territories. On April 1, 1999, the Northwest Territories was divided into two parts. The new area to the east was called Nunavut.

Nunavut has the largest land area in Canada. It is almost 2 000 000 square kilometres in area and makes up 1/5 of Canada. Its capital, Iqaluit, has a population of about 6500. Some villages in Nunavut have as few as 18 residents.

Because much of Nunavut is above the Arctic Circle, winter lasts about nine months and is extremely cold. Most of Nunavut's soil is called "permafrost", which means that it stays frozen all year round.

Most people in Nunavut are Inuit. In the Inuktitut language, Inuit means "people". People use snowmobiles and planes to travel around in Nunavut. In the old days, the Inuit used dogsleds as the main form of transportation.

The seal was the most important animal to the Inuit. They made boots from sealskin and used the blubber for both lamp oil and food. A favourite food was "muktuk" – the blubber from whales. Today, half the population still hunt and fish for their food.

ISBN: 978-1-927042-06-9

Finding Information

A. Answer the following questions.

1. What were the two territories before the formation of Nunavut?

   _____

2. What is the capital of Nunavut?

   _____

3. Why are Nunavut's winters so cold?

   _____

4. How long does winter last in Nunavut?

   _____

5. Why is Nunavut's soil called "permafrost"?

   _____

6. What are the two methods of transportation used in Nunavut?

   _____

7. What language do the Inuit people of Nunavut speak?

   _____

8. How did the Inuit people travel in the old days?

   _____

9. Which Arctic animal was the most important to the Inuit?

   _____

10. What is "muktuk"?

   _____

ISBN: 978-1-927042-06-9

 ## Nouns

- A **common noun** is the general term for a person, an animal, a place, or a thing.

  Examples: person – boy, girl, man, woman

  animal – dog, cat, pig, lion

  place – house, school, store, building, farm

  thing – car, book, plant, bicycle, doll, computer

- A **proper noun** is the actual name of a specific person, animal, place, or thing.

  Examples: person – John A. Macdonald, Wayne Gretzky, Britney Spears

  animal – Pug, Longhair, Poodle

  place – Toronto, Rogers Centre, Royal Ontario Museum

  thing – Chrysler, Barbie Doll, Kleenex

B. Put the nouns into the correct columns.

manager   farm   Mt. Albert   stickers   Mrs. Jones

CN Tower   toy   Moon River   school

Dr. Smith   truck   Husky

Common Nouns	Proper Nouns
○	○
○	○
○	○
○	○
○	○
○	○

ISBN: 978-1-927042-06-9

Consonants

- A **consonant** is any letter that is not a vowel (a, e, i, o, u).

C. **Add consonants to the vowels below. Try to form three words for each vowel.**

1. _____ u _____

   _____ u _____

   _____ u _____

2. _____ i _____

   _____ i _____

   _____ i _____

3. _____ o _____

   _____ o _____

   _____ o _____

4. _____ oo _____

   _____ oo _____

   _____ oo _____

5. _____ e _____

   _____ e _____

   _____ e _____

6. _____ ea _____

   _____ ea _____

   _____ ea _____

Missing Consonants

D. **Solve the consonant riddles. Write the consonant letters in the spaces provided.**

1. I'm a consonant that has a buzz when I fly.   _____

2. I can do this with my eyes wide open.   _____

3. I drink this instead of coffee in the morning.   _____

4. I like this kind of soup.   _____

5. You say me when you ask for a reason.   _____

6. I'm the plural of the verb "is".   _____

7. Sometimes I mark the spot.   _____

8. I'm a blue bird and a baseball player.   _____

ISBN: 978-1-927042-06-9

What Makes up Our Universe?

Astronomers are scientists who study the universe. Some astronomers believe that at one time, all the stars and planets were one big lump. They think that the universe began as a result of a big explosion that happened about 15 billion years ago. They call this event the Big Bang.

It is thought that this explosion sent pieces of the universe flying off in various directions. As time passed, some of these pieces drifted together and formed galaxies. These galaxies continue to travel in space, making the universe bigger and bigger as time passes.

Astronomers have different ideas about the future of the universe. Some believe that it will continue to grow. Others think that the galaxies will drift back towards one another, reversing the Big Bang.

We live in a galaxy called the Milky Way. When you look at the sky on a clear night, you can see the stars and planets that make up the Milky Way. The Milky Way got its name because it looks like a white stream of light. There are about 1000 billion stars in the Milky Way but we cannot see most of them.

It is believed that there are 100 billion galaxies in the universe. It is impossible to know how many billions of stars make up the entire universe. However, astronomers think that there are about 100 million trillion!

ISBN: 978-1-927042-06-9

Matching Facts

A. Do the matching.

Column A

1. Milky Way _____
2. galaxy _____
3. astronomers _____
4. 1000 billion _____
5. Big Bang _____
6. 100 billion _____

Column B

A. happened 15 billion years ago

B. the galaxy that we live in

C. number of stars in the Milky Way

D. scientists who study the universe

E. number of galaxies in the universe

F. a collection of stars and planets

Recalling Details

B. Answer the following questions.

1. Explain the Big Bang theory in your own words.

_____

_____

_____

2. How did the Milky Way get its name?

_____

_____

_____

ISBN: 978-1-927042-06-9

 Plural Nouns

- To make a noun plural, usually you can simply add "s". However, some nouns require changes and different plural endings. The rules of plural nouns are:

  1. Single nouns – just add "s"
  2. Nouns ending in "s", "z", "ch", "sh", and "x" – add "es"
  3. Nouns ending in "y" – change the "y" to "i" and add "es"
  4. Nouns ending in "f" or "fe" – change the "f" or "fe" to "v" and add "es"
  5. Nouns ending in "o" – add either "s" or "es" (depending on the word)
  6. Some nouns stay the same.
  7. Some nouns change in the middle.

C. Circle the correct plural form of each word. State which rule you are following by writing the number of the rule.   **Rule**

1.	planet	planetes	planets	planeties
2.	fox	foxes	foxen	foxs
3.	knife	knives	knifes	knifies
4.	potato	potatos	potatoes	potatose
5.	goose	gooses	geeses	geese
6.	boot	boots	beets	booties
7.	foot	fots	feet	footies
8.	half	halfs	halves	halfies
9.	galaxy	galaxies	galaxys	galaxyies
10.	moose	moose	mooses	meese

ISBN: 978-1-927042-06-9

Vowels

- The **vowels** – a, e, i, o, u – can have long or short vowel sounds.
  Examples: cat – has a short vowel sound
               plate – has a long vowel sound
  Note: the long vowel sound says the name of the actual letter.

D. Underline the vowel in each word and write "short" or "long" in the space provided.

1. space _____   2. lump _____   3. side _____

4. age _____   5. stick _____   6. tone _____

7. pop _____   8. flu _____   9. hold _____

E. Can you figure out what the children are saying? Just fill in the vowels.

1. It is a b__a__tif__l d__y today.

2. Y__s, it __s. Sh__ll we go o__ts__de?

3. L__t's go to th__ p__rk.

4. Wo__ld you l__ke to c__me t__ __?

5. Th__nk yo__ f__r ask__ng m__ to jo__n you.

6. I'd l__ve to g__ to th__ p__rk. Sh__ll I br__ng
   a s__cc__r b__ll?

7. Lo__k. There's J__hn. L__t's ask h__m to come
   al__ng.

ISBN: 978-1-927042-06-9

Are We Alone in the Universe?

Is there life on other planets? It could be possible because there are other galaxies that could have a sun like ours. These planets could have water and enough warmth to allow for life to exist.

One answer to this question may lie in the large number of UFO sightings. UFO stands for "unidentified flying object". There are over 100 reported UFO sightings daily. Many of these can be explained as weather balloons, research aircraft, or reflections from the sun. Some scientists believe that many of these sightings are real UFOs. They believe that extraterrestrials (beings from other planets) are visiting us or trying to make contact with us.

There are people who believe that they have been captured by aliens. They reported that aliens came to them while they were sleeping and took them into a spaceship. None of them reported being harmed. However, none of these cases have been proven.

Perhaps we are not alone. Perhaps those people who claim to have seen UFOs actually did see them. If so, there will be interesting encounters in space in the future.

ISBN: 978-1-927042-06-9

Remembering Details

A. Fill in the blanks with suitable words.

There could be life on another planet if it has a 1._____

like ours. For life to exist, a planet needs 2._____ and

3._____ .   Every day, there are over 4._____

reports from people who think that they have seen an

unidentified flying object. A being from another planet is

called an 5._____ . These beings would probably travel

in 6._____ . Some people believe that they have been

7._____ by aliens but they were not 8._____ .

An Interview with an Alien

> *You might use "Who / What / Where / When / Why" to make questions.*

B. Pretend that you are interviewing an alien. Write the questions that you want to ask your alien visitor. Then draw the alien.

Question 1. _____

_____

Question 2. _____

_____

Question 3. _____

_____

Question 4. _____

A Picture of My Alien

_____

ISBN: 978-1-927042-06-9

 Pronouns

- **Pronouns** *are words that are used in place of nouns.*

    Examples: 1. <u>Jennifer</u> was late for school.   <u>She</u> was late for school.
    2. <u>Denise and Paula</u> sang a song.   <u>They</u> sang a song.
    3. <u>Brian and I</u> went to the store.   <u>We</u> went to the store.
    4. Please give this book to <u>Sam</u>.   Please give this book to <u>him</u>.

    In each example above, the first underlined word is a noun, and the second is the pronoun replacing the noun.

C.   Underline the pronouns in the sentences.

The number at the end of each sentence tells you how many pronouns to find.

1.   Jeff and I went cycling together. (1)

2.   She helped him with the homework. (2)

3.   The car would not start, so we had it repaired. (2)

4.   We saw them running to catch the bus. (2)

5.   They showed me some pictures of UFOs. (2)

D.   Fill in the blanks with the correct pronouns.

1.   We/Us _____ are going to walk home together.

2.   Me/I _____ like eating popcorn at the movies.

3.   Him/He _____ is in my class.

4.   She/Her _____ is my best friend.

5.   Paul tossed she/me _____ the basketball.

ISBN: 978-1-927042-06-9

The Silent "e" and the Long Vowel

- When we add a silent "e" to a word, the vowel in the word changes from short to long.

  Example: The name "Tim", which has the short vowel sound ĭ, changes to the long vowel sound ī in the word "time".

  Notice that this little change also changes the whole meaning of the word. Instead of the name "Tim", we now have the word "time".

E. **Drop the silent "e" in the underlined words. Match the new words with the appropriate meanings.**

The Camping Trip

Last summer, our family went camping. We found a spot under a <u>huge</u> <u>pine</u> tree and pitched our tent. After the work, we had a <u>bite</u> to eat. We <u>ate</u> sandwiches and <u>ripe</u> apples. We decided to <u>use</u> the branches of the trees to hang up our towels. We saw a <u>cute</u> chipmunk and watched it <u>hide</u> behind a leaf. We used <u>tape</u> to hang up our garbage bag. We ate an ice <u>cube</u> to cool off. At night we <u>made</u> a <u>fire</u>.

1. slice in two   – _____
2. you and me   – _____
3. just a little, a – _____
4. tear   – _____
5. touch lightly – _____
6. needle and   – _____
7. shows where – _____
8. angry   – _____
9. a baby bear – _____
10. a type of tree – _____
11. could not be seen – _____
12. wrap your arms around – _____

ISBN: 978-1-927042-06-9

The sunflower plant is a very <u>attractive</u> yellow flower. It gets its name from its yellow sun-like face and also from the ability to <u>rotate</u> its face toward the sun as the sun moves from east to west during the day. With <u>plenty</u> of sun and water, the sunflower can grow over ten feet high.

Sunflowers

The sunflower is so <u>pretty</u> that it is often used in flower arrangements. It has been painted by many artists too. Even the <u>famous</u> artist Vincent Van Gogh did a series of sunflower paintings. The sunflower design is often used in arts and crafts and even fabric for clothing.

However, the sunflower is more than a pretty yellow flower. It is an important farm crop and provides food for people and wildlife. Sunflower seeds are used as a snack food. Birds love sunflower seeds and many people buy black oil sunflower seeds for their bird feeders.

The most important use of the sunflower crop is for sunflower oil, which is <u>extracted</u> from sunflower seeds. Sunflower oil is used for salad dressings, frying, and baking.

So you can see that the sunflower is a beautiful plant and also an <u>excellent</u> <u>source</u> of food.

ISBN: 978-1-927042-06-9

 **Recalling Facts**

A. Circle the correct answer to complete each of the following statements.

1. The sunflower is _____ in colour.

   A. white   B. red   C. yellow

2. The sunflower can rotate its face _____ the sun.

   A. away from   B. toward   C. around

3. The sunflower needs _____ to grow.

   A. sun and oil   B. sun and water   C. water and crop

4. The sunflower can grow to _____ tall.

   A. five feet   B. eight feet   C. ten feet

5. Sunflower oil is extracted from the _____ of sunflowers.

   A. seeds   B. flowers   C. leaves

6. Sunflower oil is used _____ .

   A. as snack food and salad dressings

   B. for baking, frying, and feeding birds

   C. for baking, frying, and as salad dressings

7. Many people use the sunflower in _____ .

   A. paintings and flower arrangements

   B. producing yellow dye for fabric

   C. fences and paintings

ISBN: 978-1-927042-06-9

Articles

- **A**, **an**, and **the** are articles.

  A is used before a word that begins with a consonant.

  An is used before a word that begins with a vowel.

  The is used before a noun that names a particular person, animal, place, or thing.

B. Use "a" or "an" before each noun.

1. _____ sunflower

2. _____ artist

3. _____ emperor

4. _____ merchant

5. _____ octopus

6. _____ sample

7. _____ ostrich

8. _____ piece

9. _____ ice cube

10. _____ umbrella

C. Complete each of the following sentences with "a", "an", or "the".

1. Sunflowers can rotate to face _____ sun.

2. I would like to travel around _____ world.

3. There is _____ interesting-looking flower in _____ garden.

4. _____ weather today is hot and humid.

5. _____ food in the fridge is still fresh.

6. _____ stranger looked suspicious.

7. Just then, I saw _____ police car pass by.

8. We bought _____ tie for Dad on Father's Day.

ISBN: 978-1-927042-06-9

 **Crossword Puzzle**

D. Use the underlined words in the passage on page 14 to solve the puzzle.

Across

A. eye-catching

B. nice-looking

C. where something is obtained

D. very good

Down

1. well-known

2. turn

3. lots of

4. taken out

ISBN: 978-1-927042-06-9

Using Magnets

Magnets are objects that can attract other objects containing iron, steel, or nickel. We can use them in many different ways.

We have all seen how magnetic strips can stick to our fridge at home or a blackboard or whiteboard at school. Fridge magnets come in thousands of designs and many people collect them for fun. They are used for advertising and displaying printed business names and phone numbers. At school, teachers use magnetic strips to hold up signs and magnetic letters for teaching young children.

Magnets are used in toys such as fishing games, building activities, and even board games. Some children have their own horseshoe magnets or a set of bar magnets to play with. These magnets can provide children with lots of fun while they learn about the science of magnetism.

Have you ever noticed how magnets are used to keep windows or doors tightly closed? Since magnets can be made very large and very strong, they are also important in industry. Factories and construction equipment use magnets in their machinery.

A very important use of magnets is for making compasses. A compass is made from a bar magnet that is free to rotate in a case. The magnetic needle in a compass will always point north, so people can use this needle to check their direction. A compass can be a small toy for children or a complicated instrument for a large ship.

As you can see, magnets are used for fun, for building, and for navigation. They are very interesting and useful in our daily lives.

ISBN: 978-1-927042-06-9

Recalling Facts

A. Write "T" for true statements and "F" for false ones.

1. Sometimes a business will use a magnetic strip to advertise its phone number. _____

2. Magnets are always small in size. _____

3. Some people like to collect fridge magnets for fun. _____

4. A compass is used to check direction. _____

5. The magnetic needle in a compass will always point toward the west. _____

6. Children should never use magnets. _____

B. Describe briefly how magnets are used in the following areas.

1. teaching   : _____

_____

2. business   : _____

_____

3. games   : _____

_____

4. factories   : _____

_____

5. navigation : _____

_____

ISBN: 978-1-927042-06-9

Unit 5

Possessive Nouns

- A **possessive noun** shows ownership.

  Example: If John owns a bicycle, you might state:

  This is John's bicycle.

- Notice that to show ownership, you add an apostrophe (') and the letter "**s**".

- Here are three important rules of possessive nouns:

  1. If the noun is singular, add "'**s**" – The boy's baseball...
  2. If the noun ends in the letter "**s**", add "'**s**" – The actress's part in the play...
  3. If the noun is plural, that is, it has an "**s**" already added to make it plural, add only the apostrophe (') – The horses' hooves could be heard in the distance...

C. Write " 's " or " ' " to make the nouns possessive.

Example: Here is Paul＿＿ coat. ⟶ Here is Paul＿'s＿ coat.

1. Julie＿＿＿ fridge magnet is cute.

2. The little alien＿＿＿ neck is very long.

3. These are aliens＿＿＿ spaceships.

4. James＿＿＿ team won the game.

5. Jim＿＿＿ dog followed him to school.

6. They played in the children＿＿＿ yard.

7. The ladies＿＿＿ fitting room is over there.

8. The coaches＿＿＿ whistles blew at the same time.

9. The coach was happy with the team＿＿＿ performance.

10. At school, there is a boys＿＿＿ washroom on the first floor.

11. The girls＿＿＿ cheers were heard throughout the gymnasium.

12. One girl＿＿＿ scream could be heard above all the rest.

ISBN: 978-1-927042-06-9

Rhyming Words

D. **Make rhyming words with the same vowel sound in each group. Use the clues to help you.**

1. **kept**

_____ went slowly

_____ cried

_____ went to bed

2. **otter**

_____ more heat

_____ goes with "fly"

_____ Harry's last name

3. **drift**

_____ a present

_____ to pick up

_____ quick or rapid

4. **ore**

_____ noise when sleeping

_____ a job around the house

_____ a place to buy things

5. **cow**

_____ above your eye

_____ at this time

_____ work in the field

6. **giver**

_____ a body organ

_____ flowing water

_____ shake when cold

7. **chew**

_____ make coffee

_____ took to the air

_____ sticky stuff

8. **feet**

_____ tidy

_____ make something hot

_____ candy

ISBN: 978-1-927042-06-9

There is nothing quite as fun and refreshing as a cool dip in the water on a hot, <u>humid</u> summer day. However, playing in water can be <u>dangerous</u> if you don't know the rules of water safety.

The first <u>rule</u> of water safety is to always swim with a <u>buddy</u>. If you have a problem, the friend can help you or run to get help. Besides, it is always more fun if you have a friend to play with. It is best to have an adult present, especially if you are not a good swimmer. Never swim at a beach where there is no lifeguard or adult present.

Swimming pools are usually well <u>supervised</u> but you can still get injured. Most injuries are a result of children running and slipping on wet pool <u>surfaces</u>. If you are a beginning swimmer, always stay in the shallow end.

If you swim in a river or lake, be sure to <u>investigate</u> what is below the water surface. If you jump or dive into unknown waters, you may seriously injure yourself on a hidden object. If you go boating, always wear a life jacket.

Water Safety

Swimming and boating are among the most <u>enjoyable</u> summer activities. Protect yourself by following these basic rules of safety.

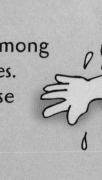

ISBN: 978-1-927042-06-9

Summarizing Information

A. In the passage, there are six rules of safety. Write each rule in your own words.

Rule #1: _____

_____

Rule #2: _____

_____

Rule #3: _____

_____

Rule #4: _____

_____

Rule #5: _____

_____

Rule #6: _____

_____

B. Pretend that you are a lifeguard at the local swimming pool. Make a sign with important safety rules. Give your sign a catchy title.

ISBN: 978-1-927042-06-9

 Possessive Adjectives

- A **possessive adjective** can replace a possessive noun to show ownership.
  Example: This is Jack's cap. This is his cap.

C. Circle the correct possessive adjectives.

1. Michael puts (his / her) life jacket away.

2. Clare swam with (her / their) friends in the pool.

3. Mom had (its / her) hair permed yesterday.

4. We take (your / our) own lunch to the park.

5. My cat likes licking (their / its) tail.

6. I always have (our / my) breakfast at home.

7. The ducklings follow (their / its) mother to cross the road.

8. I will call you tonight. Can you give me (your / my) telephone number?

D. Fill in the blanks with the correct possessive adjectives.

my	your	our	their
	his	her	its

1. Have you seen Bob's cat. _____ cat is missing.

2. We all like _____ teacher very much.

3. I am wearing a new dress. Do you like _____ dress?

4. You have a hamster. Is that _____ hamster?

5. I have two brothers. _____ names are Joe and Rob.

6. Sophia went boating with _____ parents yesterday.

ISBN: 978-1-927042-06-9

Understanding Words in Sentences

- One way to figure out the meaning of a word is to read the sentence in which the word appears. The information in the sentence will help you understand the meaning of the word.

E. Find the words listed below in the passage on page 22. Then match the words in Column A with the meanings in Column B.

Column A

1. humid ◯
2. dangerous ◯
3. rule ◯
4. buddy ◯
5. supervised ◯
6. surfaces ◯
7. investigate ◯
8. enjoyable ◯

Column B

A. best friend
B. watched
C. tops of things
D. hot and sticky
E. fun
F. not safe
G. thing to obey
H. find out about

Vowels

F. Answer the questions.

1. Three words above have four vowels. Can you list these words?

    a. _____ b. _____ c. _____

2. Which word has five vowels? _____

ISBN: 978-1-927042-06-9

Not all inventions were meant to happen. In some cases, people made mistakes that ended up becoming useful or interesting inventions.

The Popsicle was the result of a mistake. In 1905, an 11-year-old boy named Frank Epperson was trying to make a flavourful drink. He mixed soda pop powder with water and left it on his back porch overnight. It froze with the stir stick stuck in the middle. The next day he pulled it out and tasted the frozen drink. It was an instant hit. He called it the "Epperson Icicle" and sold them in his neighbourhood for five cents each. He later named the invention "Popsicle".

Accidental INVENTIONS

A year before the invention of the Popsicle, the ice cream cone was invented. One very hot afternoon at the 1904 St. Louis World's Fair, a young man was selling a lot of ice cream. Soon he ran out of paper ice cream cups. He was desperate to find something in which to serve his ice cream. Then he noticed an Arab vendor selling wafer-like biscuits sprinkled with sugar. He bought a stack of these wafers and put ice cream inside them. He sold his ice cream on the cone-like wafers. This new way to serve ice cream soon became very popular.

Both these cases prove that the old expression "Necessity is the Mother of Invention" is certainly true.

ISBN: 978-1-927042-06-9

Understanding Story Ideas

A. Write what you think the expression "*Necessity is the Mother of Invention*" means.

Sometimes there is a reason we invent things.

_____

_____

Using Facts to Make Inferences

The term "entrepreneur" refers to a person who comes up with a new business from a good idea or something that he or she invented.

B. Answer the following questions.

1. Why can we say that Frank Epperson was an "entrepreneur"?

_____

2. How was the invention of the ice cream cone an accident?

_____

3. Are you an inventor? Do you have a great idea for something new? Describe your invention and draw a picture of it.

Name of invention: _____

What it is made of: _____

What it does: _____

Who would use it: _____

_____

How much it would
cost: _____

ISBN: 978-1-927042-06-9

Verbs

- A **verb** is an action word in a sentence. It shows what the subject of the sentence is doing.

  Example: The boy ran home. "Ran" is the verb in this sentence.

C. Underline the verb in each sentence below.

1. The player dropped his stick.

2. The player shot the puck at the net.

3. The goalie fell to the ice.

4. The coach encouraged the team.

5. The player raised his arms in celebration.

6. The crowd cheered wildly.

7. A vendor sold ice cream at the arena.

D. Choose a verb that would make sense for each sentence below. Try not to use the same verb twice.

> dribbled   helped   called   swung   played
> danced   bounced   chased   gathered   moved

1. The students _____ in the schoolyard.

2. They _____ on the monkey bars.

3. Some boys _____ basketball.

4. Some of the girls _____ the younger students.

5. A few children _____ balls.

6. The teacher _____ everyone to return to class.

ISBN: 978-1-927042-06-9

Digraphs

- **Digraphs** *are two letters that, when placed together, make a single sound.*

  Examples: 1. *rain* — *the "ai" gives the sound of a long* ā.

  play — *the "ay" gives the sound of a long* ā.

  2. *feed* — *the "ee" gives the sound of a long* ē.

  each — *the "ea" gives the sound of a long* ē.

  3. *boat* — *the "oa" gives the sound of a long* ō.

E. Unscramble the mixed-up letters to make proper words.

All of these have digraphs. Put those letters together first and the rest is easy.

1. e r a h c   <u>r e a c h</u>   stretch your arm out

2. e c a r m   __ __ __ __ __   white and smooth

3. a t m e   __ __ __ __   put it on the barbecue

4. m e t a   __ __ __ __   all the players together

5. o t a c   __ __ __ __   goes with the hat

6. y t a s   __ __ __ __   don't go

7. i s l a   __ __ __ __   you need a boat

8. i t b a   __ __ __ __   fish can get hooked on this

9. t e m e   __ __ __ __   get together with a friend

10. o t s a t   __ __ __ __ __   a quick breakfast

11. e d s e   __ __ __ __   a plant grows from this

ISBN: 978-1-927042-06-9

The most popular drink in the world is, of course, water. But what is the second most popular drink? If you guessed milk, you would be wrong. It is tea.

Tea was invented about 4700 years ago. A Chinese emperor, Shen Nung, was boiling water under a tree when a few leaves fell into his drink. He noticed a pleasant smell coming from the cup. He tasted it, and from that moment on, tea became a drink.

The Second Most
Popular Drink
in the World

Tea became popular in Europe in 1610. Up until about 200 years ago, tea was actually used for money in some Asian countries. People would buy things with a block of tea or carve off a piece of the block for smaller, less expensive purchases.

The most popular form of tea is the tea bag. It was invented by Thomas Sullivan, a tea and coffee merchant. One day, he decided to send samples of tea wrapped in little silk bags to his customers. Much to his surprise, when the orders arrived for his tea, his customers insisted that the tea be wrapped in these little silk bags. The idea of the tea bag was born. Today, more than half the tea in the world is bought this way.

Each year, there are over 800 billion cups of tea consumed worldwide. Perhaps, if Thomas Sullivan had not accidentally invented the tea bag, tea would not have been so popular.

ISBN: 978-1-927042-06-9

Choosing Correct Statements

A. **In each group, put a check mark ✔ beside the correct statement. First, answer the questions without looking back at the passage. Then, reread the passage to check your answers.**

1. A. The most popular drink in the world is water. _____
   B. The most popular drink in the world is tea. _____
   C. The most popular drink in the world is milk. _____

2. A. An emperor of China discovered tea. _____
   B. The queen of England discovered tea. _____
   C. An ancient king discovered tea. _____

3. A. Tea was also used for growing plants. _____
   B. Tea was also used as money. _____
   C. Tea was also used as decoration. _____

4. A. Thomas Sullivan, who invented tea bags, was a merchant. _____
   B. Thomas Sullivan, who invented tea bags, was a sailor. _____
   C. Thomas Sullivan, who invented tea bags, was an explorer. _____

5. A. The first tea bag was made of cloth. _____
   B. The first tea bag was made of paper. _____
   C. The first tea bag was made of silk. _____

6. A. Tea was invented 4700 years ago. _____
   B. Tea was invented 800 billion years ago. _____
   C. Tea was invented 2700 years ago. _____

ISBN: 978-1-927042-06-9

Verb Tenses

- Verbs change according to which time period they are in.

  Examples: I walk. I am walking. – **present time**

  I walked. I did walk. I was walking. – **past time**

  I will walk. I shall walk. – **future time**

B.   Write the missing verb tenses in the chart below.

	Present	Past	Future
1.	drink		
2.		ran	
3.	think		
4.			will fight
5.	try		
6.			will swim

C.   Fill in the blanks with the correct form of the verbs in parentheses.

1.   Tea (become) _____ popular long ago.

2.   Susan (try) _____ the new tea bags tomorrow.

3.   Oscar (work) _____ on the project last night.

4.   They (fly) _____ the kite when the wind comes up.

5.   She (walk) _____ home with her friends every day.

6.   His parents (take) _____ a holiday next summer.

7.   He usually (go) _____ shopping on weekends.

8.   I (meet) _____ Jason this morning on my way to school.

ISBN: 978-1-927042-06-9

Consonant Blends

- A **consonant blend** is formed when two consonants form a blended sound.

D. Read the hints. Fill in the blanks with the correct consonant blends.

bl cl sm br sp cr st tr

1. __ __ e e d after a cut	2. __ __ u e s help solve puzzles
3. __ __ i n turn fast	4. __ __ a r in the night sky
5. __ __ i c k or treat	6. __ __ a b crawls underwater
7. __ __ i c k for building	8. __ __ a l l not big

E. Build rhyming words using consonant blends.

 beach   walk   fast   lick

1. _____   2. _____   3. _____   4. _____

 skim   stay   snore   spill

5. _____   6. _____   7. _____   8. _____

ISBN: 978-1-927042-06-9

Dinosaurs roamed the Earth over 200 million years ago. About 70 million years ago, they completely disappeared. We learn about dinosaurs from fossils. Fossils are found in rocks.

Rocks tell the story of the Earth's history. If we look at the edge of a cliff, we will notice that there are many layers of rock. These layers may be of different colours and thicknesses. In between these layers of rock, the skeleton remains of animals were pressed. As years passed and more rock layers piled up, these remains became impressions in the rock. It is these impressions that tell us about the dinosaur.

Fossils – the Link to the Dinosaur

The type of rock layer will reveal the time period in the Earth's history. The fossil will show the kind of animal that lived in that time because the skeleton remains were embedded there. From both these facts, we can trace the time period in which a certain animal lived. Leaf fossils found in rocks tell us what plants covered the Earth at certain time periods. Therefore, we can also figure out the plant life that the dinosaur would have depended on for food.

To understand fossils, think of a fresh piece of sidewalk concrete. If you walked on it, you would create the shape of your feet and the length of your step. If thousands of years from now, someone found your footprints in this concrete slab, what would they be able to figure out about you? They would know your shoe size, your height, your weight, and how you walked. This is the same way fossils tell the tale of dinosaurs.

ISBN: 978-1-927042-06-9

The Main Idea of a Paragraph

- **The main idea of a paragraph** is the most important fact or idea that the paragraph tells us.

A. Put a check mark ✔ in the space beside the statement that tells the main idea of each paragraph from the passage.

Paragraph One

A. Dinosaurs roamed the Earth. _____

B. We learn about dinosaurs from fossils. _____

C. Dinosaurs are extinct. _____

Paragraph Two

A. The Earth is rocky. _____

B. There are many layers of rock in a cliff. _____

C. Skeletal impressions tell us about dinosaur history. _____

Paragraph Three

A. Fossils tell us about both plant and animal lives from the past. _____

B. Leaves can be fossils, too. _____

C. Dinosaurs ate plants. _____

Paragraph Four

A. Concrete is like a layer of rock. _____

B. Fossils are like footprints in concrete. _____

C. Wet concrete leaves marks. _____

ISBN: 978-1-927042-06-9

 **Unit 9**

 Adjectives

- **Adjectives** *are words that describe nouns. They tell something about a noun and help us know more about the noun they are describing.*

   Example: *The* <u>playful</u> *kitten jumped up.*
   "Playful" is an adjective that describes the kitten.

B.   Underline the adjectives in the following sentences.

1.   The old fossils found on the historical site tell us about the extinct dinosaurs. (3)

2.   Wear a warm hat and a winter coat. (2)

3.   Wild animals belong in their natural habitat. (2)

4.   Old Mr. Smith still plays a good round of golf. (2)

5.   The dark night frightened the young children. (2)

The number following each sentence tells how many adjectives are in the sentence.

Using Adjectives

C.   Fill in the blanks with the correct adjectives.

| excited | birthday | icy | furry | cold | different | white |

1.   The rock layers are in _____ colours.

2.   The _____ steps were slippery.

3.   A _____ wind blew as the _____ snow fell.

4.   The _____ child opened her _____ gifts.

5.   The _____ dog sheds hair on the furniture.

ISBN: 978-1-927042-06-9

Consonant Blends with Three Letters

- *Some **consonant blends** are made up of three consonants placed together.*

D. Write the three-letter consonant blends to complete the words below. Use the clues to help you.

1. __ __ __ e a d	put butter on your bread
2. __ __ __ e a m	a small river
3. __ __ __ e a m	a frightful sound
4. __ __ __ e w	tossed the ball
5. __ __ __ a w	use it with a drink
6. __ __ __ i t	divide into groups
7. __ __ __ e e t	where you live
8. __ __ __ i n g	found in a mattress

Triple Consonant Crossword

E. Solve the crossword puzzle.

Across

A. a red fruit
B. a way to cook eggs

Down

1. pull apart
2. wipe clean

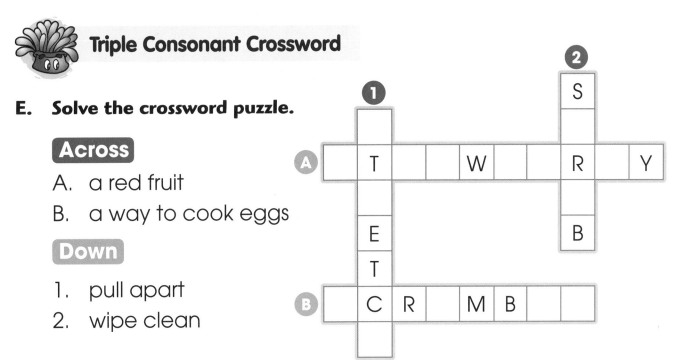

ISBN: 978-1-927042-06-9

If you are a superstitious person, you probably believe in bad luck and will do certain things to prevent bad things from happening to you.

Did you know that walking under a ladder was bad luck? This superstition

Are You Superstitious?

began many years ago when criminals were hanged in public. The ladder that led to the scaffold was a symbol of death. You may see someone knock on wood for good luck. Long ago, it was believed that gods lived in trees and if you knocked on the tree, the god would be happy and take care of you.

Breaking a mirror is supposed to bring seven years of bad luck. This idea came from the belief that the image in the mirror was actually a person's soul. If the mirror broke, the soul would be lost forever.

The day when people are most superstitious is Friday the 13th. The fact that Jesus Christ died on a Friday and that there were 13 men at the Last Supper could be reasons for this belief. Another might be that Friday was called "hangman's day", a day when criminals were executed.

Whether you are superstitious or not shouldn't matter as long as you keep your fingers crossed.

ISBN: 978-1-927042-06-9

Recalling Details

A. Write "T" for true statements and "F" for false ones.

1. Walking under a ladder is bad luck because something could fall on your head. _____

2. Superstitious people believe in bad luck. _____

3. Long ago, people believed that gods lived in trees. _____

4. Knocking on wood would bring you good luck. _____

5. Breaking a mirror may bring 20 years of bad luck. _____

6. The most superstitious day is the 13th of each month. _____

7. Friday was commonly known as "hangman's day". _____

8. A person's soul was thought to be reflected in a mirror. _____

9. Keeping your fingers crossed is supposed to bring good luck. _____

B. Match the superstitious beliefs.

Superstition	Belief
1. black cat ◯	A. Don't step on it.
2. crack in the sidewalk ◯	B. Say this after a person sneezes.
3. Bless you. ◯	C. It brings bad luck if it crosses your path.

ISBN: 978-1-927042-06-9

 Adverbs

- An **adverb** describes the verb (action word) in a sentence. It tells something about the verb, such as how an action takes place. Adverbs often end in "ly".

C. **Fill in the blanks with the correct adverbs that describe the verbs in the paragraph.**

The Basketball Game

The players leaped (high, low) 1._____ at centre court for the jump ball to start the game. The Raptors player (skilfully, carelessly) 2._____ dribbled the ball past the defensive player. He jumped in the air and shot the ball (directly, nearly) 3._____ at the basket. The ball did not go in and the Grizzlies (noisily, quickly) 4._____ grabbed the rebound. The Raptors player (slowly, cleverly) 5._____ stole the ball from the opposition and ran (swiftly, smartly) 6._____ down the court. The referee blew his whistle (loudly, softly) 7._____ and the game immediately stopped. The fans booed the referee (loudly, quietly) 8._____ when he called a foul on the Raptors player.

ISBN: 978-1-927042-06-9

Compound Words

- A **compound word** is formed when two words are put together to make a new word.

  Example: fire + place = fireplace

D. **Match the words from Balloon A with those from Balloon B to make new words. Write your new words in the spaces below.**

Use the clues to figure out the combinations.

A

basket   rain
jelly   over
play   out
photo   night

B

flow   mare
ball   bow
ground   fish
graph   side

1. _____ a game

2. _____ not in the house

3. _____ swings and things

4. _____ picture this

5. _____ with seven colours

6. _____ too full

7. _____ a sea creature

8. _____ bad dream

It's a very spooky place.

E. **Unscramble the compound word.**

G E R A V + R A Y D = __ R __ __ E __ __ R __

ISBN: 978-1-927042-06-9

Babies
of the Arctic

Although the Arctic is a very cold place, there is a variety of wildlife that <u>inhabits</u> the area. The walrus, the seal, and the polar bear are the better-known Arctic animals. Their babies are wrapped in fur or fat to protect them from the bitter cold.

The walrus mother feeds her baby milk for two years. To protect their babies from polar bears and killer whales, walruses stay in groups. When danger <u>appears</u>, they form a circle with their sharp tusks pointing outward to ward off the enemy. No one has ever <u>witnessed</u> a walrus birth but it is <u>believed</u> that the walrus mother gives birth on the ice <u>surface</u> or in the sea. The baby walrus is called a calf.

The seal is only a mother for ten days. Seals leave their pups to take care of themselves. At first, they cry for their mother. When they realize that she is not coming back, they dive into the sea. <u>Immediately</u>, they learn how to swim and hunt for food.

Although the polar bear is a big meat-eater, the baby polar bear is born without teeth. The cub cannot see or hear at birth and cannot even walk for a month. Since the cubs do not have enough fur to protect them from the cold, the mother <u>smothers</u> them in her coat and feeds them warm milk. The mother bear must teach the cubs everything necessary for <u>survival</u>.

Remarkably, most of these Arctic babies survive the cold and the danger of <u>predators</u> and grow to <u>adulthood</u> adding to the Arctic animal population.

ISBN: 978-1-927042-06-9

Recalling Details

A. Answer the following questions.

1. How long does the walrus mother feed her babies?

_____

2. Which Arctic animals are natural enemies of the baby walrus?

_____

3. How do walruses ward off predators?

_____

4. How long does the seal mother take care of her babies?

_____

5. Why is the polar bear cub considered completely helpless at birth?

_____

6. What does the mother polar bear do to keep her baby warm?

_____

7. What natural protection do most Arctic babies have against the cold?

_____

Your Opinion

B. Answer the question.

Three dangers that babies of the Arctic face are the cold, lack of food, and predators. Which do you think is the worst of these dangers? Give a reason for your choice.

_____

_____

ISBN: 978-1-927042-06-9

Unit 11

Contractions

- **Contractions** are single words that are formed by combining and shortening two words.

  Examples: can + not = cannot ⟶ can't

  I + will   = I'll

  Note the use of the apostrophe to replace letters.

C. Form contractions from the following pairs of words.

1.	she will	= _____	2.	he had	= _____
3.	we are	= _____	4.	you are	= _____
5.	were not	= _____	6.	who is	= _____
7.	did not	= _____	8.	has not	= _____
9.	I am	= _____	10.	that is	= _____
11.	have not	= _____	12.	would not	= _____
13.	is not	= _____	14.	there is	= _____

Be Creative

You may write about Arctic animals.

D. Use five of the contractions in (C) to make sentences of your own.

1. _____

2. _____

3. _____

4. _____

5. _____

ISBN: 978-1-927042-06-9

Building Vocabulary

E. **Match the underlined words in the passage on page 42 with the meanings.**

Underlined Word	Meaning
1. inhabits	A. right away
2. appears	B. thought it was true
3. witnessed	C. the top of something
4. believed	D. going on living
5. surface	E. covers completely
6. immediately	F. hunters
7. smothers	G. saw it happen
8. survival	H. lives there
9. predators	I. grown-ups
10. adulthood	J. comes into view

F. **Create new words from these words by adding new beginnings or endings.**

1. survival   + ing =   _____

2. believed   + able =   _____

3. appears   + ance =   _____

4. inhabited   + un =   _____

ISBN: 978-1-927042-06-9

Trick or Treat

On Halloween night, children go trick-or-treating in their neighbourhoods. Dressed up as ghosts, skeletons, devils, and various other characters, children knock on doors to collect their treats. Seldom do they actually perform a "trick".

It is thought that trick-or-treating comes from an old English custom. On All Souls Day, poor people went begging and promised to say prayers in exchange for food. Apple bobbing, still a favourite Halloween game, was originally an ancient ceremony honouring harvest time. A Jack O'Lantern is placed on porches and windows to tell children that treats are available.

Legend has it that a man named Jack befriended the devil and so he was not accepted into heaven. But he also played tricks on the devil again and again. This made the devil very angry. So when Jack died, the devil punished him by sending him off into the dark night to roam forever. Jack then carved out a turnip and made a lantern to light his path. People began to call this ghostly figure "Jack O'Lantern".

People believed that Halloween marked the connection between the world of the living and the world of the dead. This meant that ghosts would roam the earth on this night. Some believed that these ghosts would go back to the homes they lived in before they died.

Thankfully, Halloween today is no more than a fun night when children can dress up and get a bag full of candy. We don't have to worry about ghosts. Or do we?

ISBN: 978-1-927042-06-9

Matching Facts

A. Do the matching.

Column A	Column B

1. trick-or-treating   _____

2. apple bobbing   _____

3. Jack O'Lantern   _____

4. Jack   _____

5. All Souls Day   _____

A. shows that treats are available

B. an old English custom

C. people went begging

D. honours harvest time

E. wandered the earth

B. Answer the following questions.

1. Why did Jack have to wander the earth?

_____

_____

2. Why did ghosts roam the earth on Halloween?

_____

_____

3. How do children know where they can collect treats?

_____

_____

ISBN: 978-1-927042-06-9

The Simple Sentence

- A **simple sentence** is made up of a **subject** and a **predicate**.

- The **subject** contains a noun and sometimes an adjective (a word that describes the noun).

- The **predicate** contains a verb (the action performed by the noun subject) and sometimes an adverb (a word that describes a verb).

  Example: The happy child laughed out loud.

  The subject is "the happy child". The predicate is "laughed out loud".

C. For each sentence below, draw a line between the subject and the predicate.

1. The girls went trick-or-treating.

2. His parents went out.

3. They watched television together.

4. The fast runner won the race.

5. The first person in the gym turned on the lights.

D. Complete the sentences with your own subjects or predicates.

1. _____ got many treats.

2. _____ were late for school.

3. _____ fed the monkey at the zoo.

4. _____ made some Rice Krispies.

5. The hockey players _____ .

6. The kitten _____ .

7. My father and I _____ .

8. The students in grade three _____ .

ISBN: 978-1-927042-06-9

Halloween Words

E. **Here are some familiar Halloween words. Write a Halloween story using some of these words.**

You might want to tell about a scary Halloween night that you remember. Draw a picture of your favourite Halloween costume in the box.

ghosts   scary   windy   shadows   noises   candy
skeletons   graveyard   dark   witches   bats   moon
pumpkin   screams   chills   costumes   goblins   masks

ISBN: 978-1-927042-06-9

13

Hamburger –
the Most Popular American Food

When was the last time you had a hamburger? Was there any ham in it? The word "hamburger" looks like a combination of the words "ham" and "burger". Therefore, one would naturally think that a hamburger means a burger with ham. But why is the hamburger called "hamburger" when there is no ham in it?

The word "hamburger" has nothing to do with ham. In fact, it comes from the seaport city – Hamburg in Germany. In the 1700s, during the time of American settlement, a lot of European immigrants moved to the New World. At that time, the port of Hamburg was the last piece of European soil the immigrants felt under their feet before their voyage to the unknown. Hamburger was a food that the European immigrants had on board the Hamburg-America Line.

Like the Italian immigrants that brought the pizza to America, the German immigrants brought in the hamburger. It became even more popular with the opening of the numerous fast food restaurant chains in America and all over the world. Strangely, though, the Germans did not use the name "hamburger" in their mother tongue. In German, it was called "frikadelle". Somehow, the word "hamburger" reminded them of their voyage and their homeland.

ISBN: 978-1-927042-06-9

 **Recalling Facts**

A. Circle the correct answers.

1. Hamburg is the name of a ____ .

    A. town   B. port   C. food

2. The New World refers to ____ .

    A. America   B. Europe   C. Italy

3. The early immigrants to the New World travelled by ____ .

    A. ship   B. boat   C. railroad

4. Pizzas were brought to America by the ____ .

    A. Canadians   B. Germans   C. Italians

5. "Hamburger" reminded the immigrants of their ____ .

    A. forefathers   B. early days in the New World
    C. homeland

6. "Frikadelle" is a/an ____ word.

    A. German   B. American   C. Italian

B.

Can you think of the name of another food that is as misleading as "hamburger"?

_____

ISBN: 978-1-927042-06-9

Subject-Verb Agreement

- When you write a sentence, it is important to have the **verb** agree with the **noun (subject)**.

- If the subject is singular, the verb must be in the singular form.
  If the subject is plural, the verb must be in the plural form.

C. Write the correct verb in each of the sentences.

1. The hamburger (are, is) _____ a popular American food.

2. The animals in the forest (was, were) _____ restless.

3. The students (comes, come) _____ to the gym every week.

4. Jim and Jackie (is, are) _____ cousins.

5. Paul (are, is) _____ leaving early.

Tricky Situations

- Words such as "anyone", "each", "everyone", and "no one" always use singular verbs.

- Single words that refer to groups (family, school, team) usually have singular verbs.

D. Write the correct verb in each of the sentences.

1. The soccer team (arrives, arrive) _____ today.

2. The members of the club (is, are) _____ having a meeting.

3. Everyone (is, are) _____ coming to the party.

4. Each of the boys (comes, come) _____ by car.

5. The school (was, were) _____ getting together to raise money.

ISBN: 978-1-927042-06-9

Building Vocabulary

E. Fill in the blanks with words from the passage on page 50.

1. Spanish is Mark's mother _____ .

2. The early _____ mainly came from Europe.

3. The _____ to the New World was filled with danger.

4. There were a lot of people on _____ the ship.

5. "Homeland" is a _____ of the
    words "home" and "land".

**F. Create compound words with the
     words in the apples in the tree.**

board

paper

ship

coat

wood

print

1. space_____

2. news_____

3. finger_____

4. black_____

5. rain_____

6. fire_____

> A compound word is formed
> when two words are put
> together to make a new
> word.

Next time your friend tells you not to chew gum, you could say that you are exercising your jaw. That was the reason a dentist named William Semple invented gum in 1869. But his gum was not a big success because it was flavourless. People preferred to chew the gum from the spruce tree because it had a pleasant taste.

Spruce gum was scarce because spruce trees were being cut down to make paper. Later, Thomas Adams combined chicle, a rubbery sap from the sapodilla tree of

The Origin of Gum Chewing

South America, with gum to create a new flavour sensation. In 1871, Adams invented a machine that made chicle gum into sticks. He claimed that his gum could improve blood circulation, strengthen teeth, and refresh the brain.

Soon, candy-coated gum named "little chicles" came along, which became known as "Chiclets". Following the invention of Chiclets was Blibber-Blubber. It was a strong form of gum that enabled the chewer to blow bubbles. Soon, people around the world started chewing gum.

For years, students have been hiding their gum under their desks to prevent being caught chewing gum in class. An even quicker way of getting rid of the evidence is to swallow it! This may make the gum disappear quickly but it is not a good idea because gum never really gets digested properly.

ISBN: 978-1-927042-06-9

Comprehension Crossword Puzzle

A. **Solve the crossword puzzle using words from the passage.**

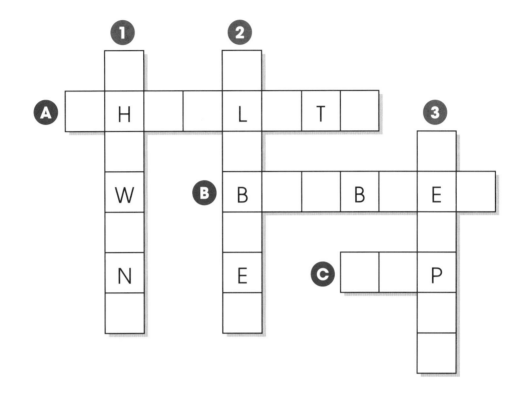

Across	Down
A. candy-coated gum	1. exercising with gum
B. what you can blow	2. goes with Blubber
C. Chicle is a rubbery form of this.	3. William's last name

Your Opinion

B. **Give two reasons for the popularity of chewing gum throughout the world.**

1. _____

2. _____

ISBN: 978-1-927042-06-9

 Types of Sentences

- **Sentences** *are written for different purposes.*
  1. An **interrogative sentence** *asks a question.*
     Example: *What time is it? (A question mark follows an interrogative sentence.)*
  2. A **declarative sentence** *makes a simple statement.*
     Example: *The boy walked his dog. (A period ends a declarative sentence.)*
  3. An **exclamatory sentence** *shows emotion.*
     Example: *Look out for the car! (An exclamatory sentence is followed by an exclamation mark.)*
  4. An **imperative sentence** *tells what you want to happen.*
     Example: *Wait until you're called. (An imperative sentence is followed by a period.)*

C. **Punctuate each sentence and state the type of sentence (interrogative, declarative, exclamatory, imperative) in the space provided.**

At the Baseball Game

At a professional baseball game, exciting things happen.

1. Take your seats before the game begins _____

2. Which team is winning so far _____

3. The bases are loaded _____

4. Wow, what a great catch _____

5. Is the runner fast enough to steal a base _____

D. **Pretend you are at the game. Make up four sentences about the game.**

1. Interrogative _____

2. Declarative _____

3. Exclamatory _____

4. Imperative _____

ISBN: 978-1-927042-06-9

Homophones

- **Homophones** are words that sound the same but are spelled differently.

  Example: hear   here

  I could not <u>hear</u> what he said.   He was <u>here</u> on time.

E.   Fill in the blank with the correct word in each pair of homophones.

> Use a dictionary if you are not sure which word to use.

1. James has   bean/been   _____ to school every day.

2. My   father/farther   _____ works downtown.

3. I would/wood _____ like to travel.

4. She looked pale/pail _____ because she was ill.

5. All weak/week _____ we have to go to school.

6. The hair/hare _____ beat the tortoise in a race.

7. I could not stop my bicycle because the brake/break _____ did not work.

8. The cake was made out of flower/flour _____ .

9. The made/maid _____ cleaned the hotel room.

10. We had to weight/wait _____ in line.

11. The turtle fell into the hole/whole _____ .

12. You should write/right _____ the answer in the box.

ISBN: 978-1-927042-06-9

A simple garden shows how a food chain works. Suppose you have lettuce growing in your garden. That lettuce gets energy from sunlight. It also soaks up water and nutrients from the soil. It now has everything it needs to grow. Think of this lettuce as the first link in a garden food chain.

Suppose one night a slug slithers onto the leaf of the lettuce and begins eating it. The energy from the lettuce is now transferred to the slug. The slug becomes the second link in the food chain. In the morning, a beetle comes along and eats the slug. The energy from the slug is now passed on to the beetle, which becomes the third link in the chain.

Just then, along comes a hungry shrew that eats the beetle. Now the shrew is enjoying the energy from the beetle. But the food chain is not over. A wise old owl swoops down, picks up the shrew, and returns to its nest to prepare it for dinner.

The Food Chain

The owl has no natural predators. That means that there is no animal that tries to kill the owl for food. The owl is at the top of the food chain and benefits from the energy passed through all the members of the chain – the lettuce, the slug, the beetle, and the shrew.

There are many different food chains in nature. Each environment has its own food chain. We, too, are part of a food chain. Lucky for us, like the wise old owl, we are also at the top of our chain.

ISBN: 978-1-927042-06-9

Understanding Facts

A.   Put the members of this food chain in order.

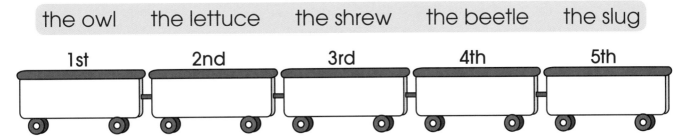

the owl   the lettuce   the shrew   the beetle   the slug

| 1st | 2nd | 3rd | 4th | 5th |

 Understanding Information

B.   Answer the following questions about the food chain.

1.   In the food chain, what is the role of the sun and the nutrients in the soil?

_____

_____

2.   What does it mean to transfer energy?

_____

_____

3.   Why do you think the owl has no natural predators?

_____

_____

4.   If we are part of a food chain, what position in the chain would we be placed?

_____

5.   Can you name three animals that would be at the top of their food chains? (not from the passage)

a. _____   b. _____   c. _____

ISBN: 978-1-927042-06-9

 Creating Simple Sentences

C. **Unscramble each group of words to make a proper sentence. Remember to look for a subject and a predicate.**

1. game   the   we   won

   _____

2. long   it   day   rained   all

   _____

3. cream   ice   he   two   ate   scoops   of

   _____

4. holidays   summer   finally   here   are

   _____

5. the   test   gave   teacher   students   a   the

   _____

6. water   the   up   plants   soil   from   soak   the

   _____

D. **Match the subjects with the predicates.**

Subject	Predicate
1. The old man	A. gathered in the school gymnasium.
2. The crying baby	B. walked with a cane.
3. The police officer	C. made a lot of noise.
4. All the students	D. chased the thief.

ISBN: 978-1-927042-06-9

Synonyms

- A **synonym** is a word that means the same as another word.

E. Complete the crossword puzzle with words that match the clues.

Try to match the synonyms in the word bank with the clue words first.

Across

A. sad
B. oceans
C. total
D. remain
E. finish

Down

1. cut
2. rude
3. dish
4. lower

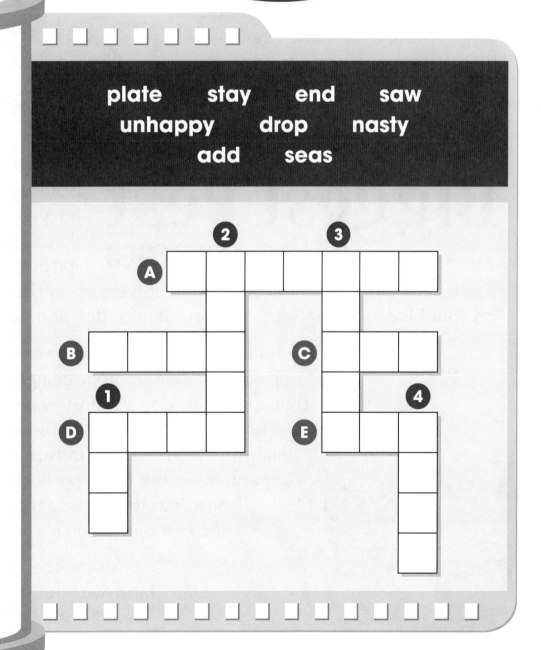

plate   stay   end   saw
unhappy   drop   nasty
add   seas

ISBN: 978-1-927042-06-9

Most people would agree that summer's biggest pest is the mosquito. This pesky little insect can quickly ruin a walk in the woods or a holiday at a cottage.

Actually, only the female mosquito bites. The male mosquito feeds on plant juices. The female mosquito drinks our blood to get protein to make eggs. One bite into your arm or leg can help the female mosquito produce 50 to 100 eggs.

The Biggest Pest
of the Summer

The mosquito has a pointed beak that sticks into your skin. Once your skin is pierced, the mosquito spits saliva into the wound to stop the blood from clotting. Then, it is easier for the mosquito to fill up on your blood. The saliva causes your skin to itch and swell up.

Some people attract mosquitoes more than others. To prevent mosquitoes from biting you, there are some things you can do. Avoid wearing dark colours and clothes made of rough materials. Blue jeans, for example, will attract mosquitoes. Don't wear perfume or use other products with strong scents. These scents attract these annoying insects. Probably the best prevention is a good insect repellent.

Mosquitoes are very sneaky. They land without a sound and weigh almost nothing. You usually notice them only after they have already enjoyed a meal of your blood.

ISBN: 978-1-927042-06-9

Checking Facts

A. Write "T" for true statements and "F" for false ones.

1. Only the male mosquito bites people. _____
2. The mosquito spits saliva into the wound when it bites. _____
3. The saliva in the wound stops blood from clotting. _____
4. There is seldom an itch after a bite. _____
5. The mosquito's saliva can stop bleeding. _____
6. All people attract mosquitoes equally. _____
7. Light-coloured clothes attract mosquitoes. _____
8. Blue jeans attract mosquitoes. _____
9. Mosquitoes do not like perfume. _____
10. Mosquitoes are noisy. _____
11. Mosquitoes are very light. _____
12. One female mosquito can produce 50 to 100 eggs. _____

Using Information

B. Answer the following questions.

1. Imagine you are at a cottage in the middle of the mosquito season. What would you do to protect yourself?

   _____

   _____

2. Explain how the mosquito sucks blood.

   _____

   _____

ISBN: 978-1-927042-06-9

Unit 16

Building Sentences with Adjectives and Adverbs

- Remember that an **adjective** describes a noun and an **adverb** describes a verb. We use adjectives and adverbs to give more information and make sentences more interesting.

C. **Rewrite the following sentences with the adjectives and adverbs provided. Add <u>both</u> words to each sentence.**

1. The boy ran. (happy, quickly)

   _____

2. The wind blew. (howling, furiously)

   _____

3. The students sang the songs. (talented, loudly)

   _____

4. The game was finished. (exciting, early)

   _____

5. John, the boy in the class, was late. (tallest, again)

   _____

D. **Add your own descriptive words to the story below.**

The 1._____ girl received a 2._____ bicycle for her birthday. She was very 3._____ to get such a 4._____ gift. She rode 5._____ down the road toward the 6._____ house of her 7._____ friend, Sarah. It was a very 8._____ day for her.

ISBN: 978-1-927042-06-9

Antonyms

- *An **antonym** is a word that has the opposite meaning of another word.*

E. **Solve the antonym word puzzles. Unscramble the antonyms and write the answers in the boxes.**

1. m e n y e	☐☐☐☐☐	friend
2. l a y p	☐☐☐☐	work
3. e f a s	☐☐☐☐	dangerous
4. d r a h	☐☐☐☐	soft
5. m a c l	☐☐☐☐	windy
6. u n i r	☐☐☐☐	repair
7. p m e y t	☐☐☐☐☐	crowded
8. k e a w	☐☐☐☐	strong

F. **Circle the antonym for each word from the choices.**

1. beautiful	ugly	happy	careful	pretty
2. funny	joking	comical	serious	laughing
3. unusual	regular	peculiar	odd	strange
4. exciting	interesting	dull	fun	scary
5. tame	soft	gentle	wild	rare

ISBN: 978-1-927042-06-9

Before winter arrives, many species of birds instinctively know that it is time to head south. The mystery of migration has always puzzled us. Why do only some birds migrate? How do birds know when to go south? How do they find their way?

Some birds fly south because their food supply runs short in winter. The woodpecker, for example, does not need to fly south because it can find food stuck in the bark of trees. The insects that the woodpecker eats are safe in the bark from the winter cold and snow.

Some birds rely on grains, shoots, insects, and other foods that disappear in winter. These birds must head south where food is still available. But why do they not stay south? Perhaps they know that if they stayed down south, they would run out of food there, too.

It is possible that birds know when winter is coming because they notice that the days are getting shorter. Once they leave from the north, they use the sun as a compass. The sun is in different positions in the sky at various times of day. In order to use it as a guide, birds would have to know the time of day. On long flights, birds use the stars to navigate their route.

The Mystery of Migration

The homing pigeon does not use the sun or the stars. Scientists believe that it uses the magnetic field of the Earth. One of the most amazing migrations is that of the tiny hummingbird. It travels from Canada to Mexico – a distance of over 3200 kilometres.

ISBN: 978-1-927042-06-9

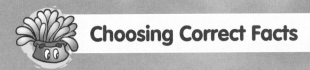

Choosing Correct Facts

A. **Place a check mark ✔ in the space beside the answer that makes the correct statement.**

1. Birds know when to fly south because
   A. they see the sunrise. _____
   B. they have good instincts. _____
   C. they follow a leader. _____

2. It is believed that birds fly south because
   A. they need food. _____
   B. they like warm weather. _____
   C. they get lost. _____

3. The woodpecker does not need to fly south because
   A. it has no instincts. _____
   B. its food is protected in the bark of trees. _____
   C. it does not know the way. _____

4. Birds do not stay south because
   A. they get too warm. _____
   B. they follow the sun. _____
   C. they do not want the food supply to run out there. _____

5. On long migration flights, birds navigate by
   A. the stars. _____
   B. other birds. _____
   C. the weather. _____

6. The homing pigeon is different because it finds its way by
   A. following the sun. _____
   B. using the magnetic field of the Earth. _____
   C. following the same route. _____

ISBN: 978-1-927042-06-9

 Capitalization

- Here are some rules of **capitalization**:
  1. Use a capital letter to begin a sentence.
  2. Use a capital letter for names (people, pets).
  3. Use a capital for the names of places on the map (cities, lakes, rivers, countries...).
  4. Use a capital for names of places and things such as buildings, companies, and historic sites.
  5. Use a capital for days of the week and months of the year.
  6. Use a capital for titles (Dr., Mr., Mrs., Miss, Ms., Prime Minister, President, Professor, Prince, Queen...).
  7. Use capitals for the words in titles of books, movies, and songs (even your own stories).

B. **There are 34 missing capitals in the story below. Write over the letters that should be capitalized in dark pen or pencil.**

> You be the teacher. Correct the words.

my trip to england

my name is billy henderson. i live at 723 main st. my dad is a doctor and his patients call him dr. henderson. this summer we are going on a holiday to england to visit my aunt, rita. aunt rita lives near the thames river. we are going to visit buckingham palace while we are there. our flight is booked on british airways and we will land at heathrow airport. we are leaving on august 11, and returning on september 3. while we are away, our neighbour, mrs. watson, will look after our dog, scamp.

ISBN: 978-1-927042-06-9

Idioms

- An **idiom** is a group of words that has a meaning other than what it really says.

- We use idioms today to get ideas across. Idioms are convenient because they are widely known and understood.

C. Here are some everyday idioms. Can you guess what they mean? Write explanations in the spaces provided.

1. "The early bird catches the worm."

   _____

2. He led me on a "wild goose chase".

   _____

3. We tried to "butter up" the teacher to get less homework.

   _____

4. When she lost her cat, she "was feeling blue".

   _____

5. The students were "in hot water" over the broken window.

   _____

6. My dad "blew his top" when he got a flat tire.

   _____

D. Write sentences using these idioms.

1. out of this world _____

2. spill the beans _____

3. going bananas _____

ISBN: 978-1-927042-06-9

The Wonderbolt Circus Show

It was the last Saturday of the summer vacation and Jennifer wanted to do something special. She heard from her friends that the Wonderbolt Circus Show was excellent, so she asked her mom and dad to take her to the show. The whole event was an exciting display of clowns, jugglers, and acrobats.

The clowns had traditional costumes with baggy pants, big shoes, and brightly coloured hats and ties. Their white faces with bright red noses and mouths made them look scary and funny at the same time.

There were three jugglers who wore shiny suits with colourful sequins. Their juggling act was awesome and they told the audience that they had gained their skills after many years of practice.

Two acrobats performed amazing tricks on the trapeze and there was also a famous handbalancer who could walk on his hands and perform upside down.

The program had information about the circus and it said that the man who started this circus had attended a famous clown college. It was the Ringling Brothers and Barnum & Bailey Clown College, which had trained clowns for many years.

All the performers were very talented and well-trained. The fantastic performances, colourful costumes, and live music made it an unforgettable experience for the whole family, and a wonderful way to end the summer vacation for Jennifer.

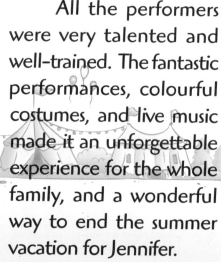

ISBN: 978-1-927042-06-9

 **Matching Facts**

A. Do the matching.

Column A	Column B

Column A

1. clowns   _____
2. jugglers   _____
3. acrobats   _____
4. handbalancer   _____
5. clown college   _____

Column B

A. performed upside down

B. where clowns are trained

C. wore shiny suits with colourful sequins

D. had white faces and red noses and mouths

E. performed on the trapeze

Recalling Details

B. Answer the following questions.

1. When did Jennifer go to the Wonderbolt Circus Show?

_____

_____

2. Why did Jennifer want to go to the Wonderbolt Circus Show?

_____

_____

3. What college did the founder of the Wonderbolt Circus Show attend?

_____

_____

ISBN: 978-1-927042-06-9

 **Letter Writing**

C. **Imagine that you are Jennifer. Write a letter to one of the performers in the Wonderbolt Circus Show.**

Think of three or four questions you might ask him or her. Try to write complete sentences with descriptive words.

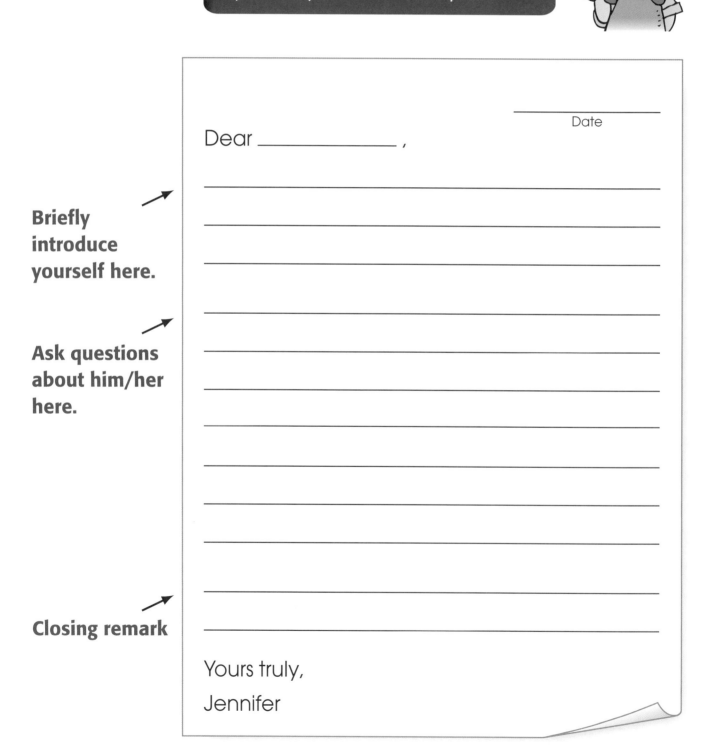

_____ Date

Dear _____ ,

Briefly introduce yourself here.

Ask questions about him/her here.

Closing remark

Yours truly,

Jennifer

ISBN: 978-1-927042-06-9

Building New Words

- **New words** are built from root words.

  Example: true → untrue truly truth

D. Circle the words in the puzzle.

happiness
harmful
finest
newest
pitiful
priceless
eventful
trapped
tossing
sadness
stopper
building

b	u	i	l	d	i	n	g	j	k
h	a	r	m	f	u	l	q	w	e
a	s	m	p	i	t	i	f	u	l
p	a	f	t	n	e	w	e	s	t
p	r	i	c	e	l	e	s	s	r
i	r	t	o	s	s	i	n	g	a
n	o	n	h	t	r	v	u	l	p
e	v	e	n	t	f	u	l	z	p
s	e	s	a	d	n	e	s	s	e
s	n	s	t	o	p	p	e	r	d

E. Write the root word of each of the words in (D).

ISBN: 978-1-927042-06-9

ISBN: 978-1-927042-06-9

Answers

1 Nunavut, Canada's Newest Territory

A.
1. They were the Yukon and the Northwest Territories.
2. It is Iqaluit.
3. Much of Nunavut is above the Arctic Circle.
4. It lasts about nine months.
5. It stays frozen all year round.
6. They are snowmobiles and planes.
7. They speak Inuktitut.
8. They travelled on dogsleds.
9. The seal was the most important Arctic animal to the Inuit.
10. It is the blubber from whales.

B. Common Nouns: manager ; farm ; stickers ; toy ; school ; truck

Proper Nouns: Mt. Albert ; Mrs. Jones ; CN Tower ; Moon River ; Dr. Smith ; Husky

C. (Individual answers)

D.
1. b
2. c
3. t
4. p
5. y
6. r
7. x
8. j

2 What Makes up Our Universe?

A.
1. B
2. F
3. D
4. C
5. A
6. E

B. (Suggested answers)
1. An explosion in the universe sent millions of particles out in space. Some of these particles drifted together and formed galaxies.
2. The Milky Way got its name because it looks like a white stream of light.

C.
1. planets ; 1
2. foxes ; 2
3. knives ; 4
4. potatoes ; 5
5. geese ; 7
6. boots ; 1
7. feet ; 7
8. halves ; 4
9. galaxies ; 3
10. moose ; 6

D.
1. space ; long
2. lump ; short
3. side; long
4. age ; long
5. stick ; short
6. tone ; long
7. pop ; short
8. flu ; long
9. hold ; long

E.
1. It is a beautiful day today.
2. Yes, it is. Shall we go outside?
3. Let's go to the park.
4. Would you like to come too?
5. Thank you for asking me to join you.
6. I'd love to go to the park. Shall I bring a soccer ball?
7. Look. There's John. Let's ask him to come along.

3 Are We Alone in the Universe?

A.
1. sun
2. water
3. warmth
4. 100
5. extraterrestrial
6. spaceships
7. captured
8. harmed

B. (Individual writing and drawing)

C.
1. I
2. She ; him
3. we ; it
4. We ; them
5. They ; me

D.
1. We
2. I
3. He
4. She
5. me

E.
1. cut
2. us
3. bit
4. rip
5. tap
6. pin
7. at
8. mad
9. cub
10. fir
11. hid
12. hug

4 Sunflowers

A.
1. C
2. B
3. B
4. C
5. A
6. C
7. A

B.
1. a
2. an
3. an
4. a
5. an
6. a
7. an
8. a
9. an
10. an

ISBN: 978-1-927042-06-9

Answers

C.
1. the
2. the
3. an ; the
4. The
5. The
6. The
7. a
8. a

D.

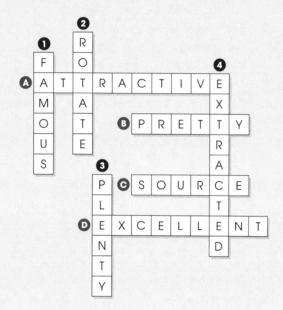

5 Using Magnets

A.
1. T
2. F
3. T
4. T
5. F
6. F

B.
1. holding up signs and magnetic letters
2. advertising and displaying names and phone numbers
3. used in fishing games, building activities, and board games
4. used in machinery
5. used in compasses to check direction

C.
1. Julie's
2. alien's
3. aliens'
4. James's
5. Jim's
6. children's
7. ladies'
8. coaches'
9. team's
10. boys'
11. girls'
12. girl's

D.
1. crept ; wept ; slept
2. hotter ; swatter ; Potter
3. gift ; lift ; swift
4. snore ; chore ; store
5. brow ; now ; plough
6. liver ; river ; shiver
7. brew ; flew ; glue
8. neat ; heat ; sweet

6 Water Safety

A. (Suggested answers)
1. Swim with a buddy.
2. Never swim at a beach with no lifeguards.
3. Do not run around in the pool area.
4. Always stay in the shallow end if you are a beginning swimmer.
5. Check below the water surface in rivers and lakes.
6. Wear a life jacket when boating.

B. (Individual drawing and writing)

C.
1. his
2. her
3. her
4. our
5. its
6. my
7. their
8. your

D.
1. His
2. our
3. my
4. your
5. Their
6. her

E.
1. D
2. F
3. G
4. A
5. B
6. C
7. H
8. E

F.
1a. dangerous
b. supervised
c. enjoyable
2. investigate

7 Accidental Inventions

A. (Suggested answer)
When something is needed, it will be invented.

B. (Suggested answers)
1. He turned an accidental invention into a business.
2. It only happened when an ice cream vendor ran out of cups and needed something to serve the ice cream.
3. (Individual answers)

ISBN: 978-1-927042-06-9

C. 1. dropped   2. shot
    3. fell   4. encouraged
    5. raised   6. cheered
    7. sold
D. (Suggested answers)
    1. gathered   2. swung
    3. played   4. helped
    5. bounced   6. called
E. 2. cream   3. meat
    4. team   5. coat
    6. stay   7. sail
    8. bait   9. meet
    10. toast   11. seed

8 The Second Most Popular Drink in the World

A. 1. A   2. A
    3. B   4. A
    5. C   6. A
B. 1. drank ; will drink
    2. run ; will run
    3. thought ; will think
    4. fight ; fought
    5. tried ; will try
    6. swim ; swam
C. 1. became
    2. will try
    3. worked
    4. will fly
    5. walks
    6. will take
    7. goes
    8. met
D. 1. bleed   2. clues
    3. spin   4. star
    5. trick   6. crab
    7. brick   8. small
E. (Suggested answers)
    1. bleach   2. stalk
    3. blast   4. stick
    5. swim   6. sway
    7. store   8. still

9 Fossils – the Link to the Dinosaur

A. Paragraph One: B
    Paragraph Two: C

Paragraph Three: A
Paragraph Four: B
B. 1. old ; historical ; extinct
    2. warm ; winter
    3. Wild ; natural
    4. Old ; good
    5. dark ; young
C. 1. different
    2. icy
    3. cold ; white
    4. excited ; birthday
    5. furry
D. 1. spread   2. stream
    3. scream   4. threw
    5. straw   6. split
    7. street   8. spring
E.

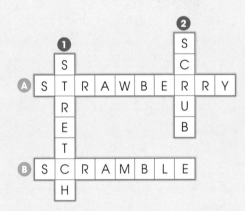

10 Are You Superstitious?

A. 1. F   2. T
    3. T   4. T
    5. F   6. F
    7. T   8. T
    9. T
B. 1. C   2. A
    3. B
C. 1. high
    2. skilfully
    3. directly
    4. quickly
    5. cleverly
    6. swiftly
    7. loudly
    8. loudly

ISBN: 978-1-927042-06-9

Answers

D.   1. basketball
     2. outside
     3. playground
     4. photograph
     5. rainbow
     6. overflow
     7. jellyfish
     8. nightmare
E.   GRAVEYARD

11   Babies of the Arctic

A.   1. She feeds them for two years.
     2. Polar bears and killer whales are natural enemies of the baby walrus.
     3. They form a circle with their tusks facing outward.
     4. She takes care of them for ten days.
     5. It cannot see, hear, or walk.
     6. She smothers the cub in her coat and feeds it warm milk.
     7. They have either fur or fat to protect them against the cold.
B.   (Individual writing)
C.   1. she'll   2. he'd
     3. we're   4. you're
     5. weren't   6. who's
     7. didn't   8. hasn't
     9. I'm   10. that's
    11. haven't   12. wouldn't
    13. isn't   14. there's
D.   (Individual writing)
E.   1. H   2. J
     3. G   4. B
     5. C   6. A
     7. E   8. D
     9. F   10. I
F.   1. surviving
     2. believable
     3. appearance
     4. uninhabited

12   Trick or Treat

A.   1. B   2. D
     3. A   4. E
     5. C
B.   (Suggested answers)
     1. Jack had to wander the earth as punishment for playing tricks on the devil.
     2. They would go back to their old homes before they died.
     3. They know they can get treats when they see Jack O'Lanterns on porches and windows.
C.   1. The girls | went trick-or-treating.
     2. His parents | went out.
     3. They | watched television together.
     4. The fast runner | won the race.
     5. The first person in the gym | turned on the lights.
D.   (Individual writing)
E.   (Individual writing and drawing)

13   Hamburger – the Most Popular American Food

A.   1. B   2. A
     3. A   4. C
     5. C   6. A
B.   (Individual writing)
C.   1. is   2. were
     3. come   4. are
     5. is
D.   1. arrives   2. are
     3. is   4. comes
     5. was
E.   1. tongue   2. immigrants
     3. voyage   4. board
     5. combination
F.   1. ship
     2. paper
     3. print
     4. board
     5. coat
     6. wood

14   The Origin of Gum Chewing

A.

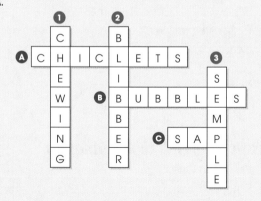

ISBN: 978-1-927042-06-9

B.   (Individual writing)

C. 1. Take your seats before the game begins. ; imperative

     2. Which team is winning so far? ; interrogative

     3. The bases are loaded. ; declarative

     4. Wow, what a great catch! ; exclamatory

     5. Is the runner fast enough to steal a base? ; interrogative

D.   (Individual writing)

E. 1. been   2. father

     3. would   4. pale

     5. week   6. hare

     7. brake   8. flour

     9. maid   10. wait

   11. hole   12. write

15   The Food Chain

A.   the lettuce ; the slug ; the beetle ; the shrew ; the owl

B.   (Suggested answers)

     1. They provide energy for the first link in the food chain.

     2. It means to pass energy from one thing to another.

     3. It can fly and no animals prey on it.

     4. We would be placed at the top of the food chain.

   5a. lion

     b. polar bear

     c. eagle

C. 1. We won the game.

     2. It rained all day long.

     3. He ate two scoops of ice cream.

     4. Summer holidays are finally here.

     5. The teacher gave the students a test.

     6. The plants soak up water from the soil.

D. 1. B   2. C

     3. D   4. A

E.

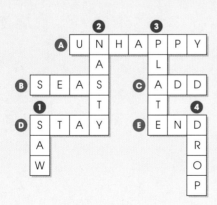

16   The Biggest Pest of the Summer

A. 1. F   2. T

     3. T   4. F

     5. F   6. F

     7. F   8. T

     9. F   10. F

   11. T   12. T

B.   (Individual writing)

C. 1. The happy boy ran quickly.

     2. The howling wind blew furiously.

     3. The talented students sang the songs loudly.

     4. The exciting game was finished early.

     5. John, the tallest boy in the class, was late again.

D.   (Individual answers)

E. 1. enemy   2. play

     3. safe   4. hard

     5. calm   6. ruin

     7. empty   8. weak

F. 1. ugly   2. serious

     3. regular   4. dull

     5. wild

17   The Mystery of Migration

A. 1. B   2. A

     3. B   4. C

     5. A   6. B

B.   My Trip to England

     My name is Billy Henderson. I live at 723 Main St. My dad is a doctor and his patients call him Dr. Henderson. This summer we are going on a holiday to England to visit my aunt, Rita. Aunt Rita lives near the Thames River. We are going to visit Buckingham Palace while we are there. Our flight is booked on British Airways and we will land at Heathrow Airport. We are leaving on August 11, and returning on September 3. While we are away, our neighbour, Mrs. Watson, will look after our dog, Scamp.

C.   (Suggested answers)

     1. If you are the first, you will win.

     2. He led me all over the place.

     3. We tried to convince the teacher to give us less homework.

     4. When she lost her cat, she was sad.

     5. The students were in trouble for breaking the window.

     6. My dad was very angry when he got a flat tire.

ISBN: 978-1-927042-06-9

D.   (Individual writing)
1.   Meaning: very special
2.   Meaning: tell everything
3.   Meaning: going crazy

18   The Wonderbolt Circus Show

A.   1. D   2. C
        3. E   4. A
        5. B

B.   1.   She went on the last Saturday of the summer vacation.
        2.   She heard from her friends that it was a good show and she wanted to do something special to end the summer vacation.
        3.   He attended a famous clown college called the Ringling Brothers and Barnum & Bailey Clown College.

C.   (Individual writing)

D.

b	u	i	l	d	i	n	g	j	k
h	a	r	m	f	u	l	q	w	e
a	s	m	p	i	t	i	f	u	l
p	a	f	t	n	e	w	e	s	t
p	r	i	c	e	l	e	s	s	r
i	r	t	o	s	s	i	n	g	a
n	o	n	h	t	r	v	u	l	p
e	v	e	n	t	f	u	l	z	p
s	e	s	a	d	n	e	s	s	e
s	n	s	t	o	p	p	e	r	d

E.   (Order may vary.)
        happy ; harm ; fine ; new ; pity ; price ; event ;
        trap ; toss ; sad ; stop ; build

ISBN: 978-1-927042-06-9